DOISNEAU
PARIS

BRIGITTE OLLIER

DOISNEAU
PARIS

Gingko
PRESS

Thanks to:
Roxanne Debuisson
Francine Deroudille
Annette Doisneau
Martine Franck
Sophie Ristelhueber
Chantal Soler
Sabine Weiss
Henri Cartier-Bresson
Raymond Grosset
Jean-Luc Mercié
Philippe Salaün

CONTENTS

On the banks of the Seine, Robert Doisneau's shadow, October 1969

AROUND PARIS, STEALTHILY

"I've never seen an eagle in my life. Only pictures. Or caged. How about you? I mean before being put on Omega.
– No, never. My memories interest you?
– …
– Yes, yes, you caught me, but I saw you coming. "

Dominique Meens, *Eux et nous*, Éditions Allia.

"It wasn't anything extraordinary but it was honest. And then, there's a certain unnamable something about hand-decorated objects. Even the most moronic workman finds a way to put a bit of himself into it. An awkward brushstroke can reveal his secret dreams. And I like morons better than machines… " This victory of man over machine, if somewhat stupidly virtuous, is one of thousands of gourmet anecdotes evoked by film-maker Jean Renoir in an impressionistic biography of his father, Pierre-Auguste Renoir (1841-1919), published at the beginning of the rock-and-rolling '60s. It's a thought that could have been voiced by Robert Doisneau (1912-1994), who worked so hard at stepping off the straight and narrow, at making his photographs "by hand", akin perhaps to baking a "home-made" cake, going his own way, preferring imperfection at all costs to even the most successful of imitations.

But since the heavenly powers chose to grant Robert Doisneau success fairly late in life, the man who created the *Baiser de l'Hôtel de Ville* didn't have time to get a big head, which in his opinion represented one of the dangers threatening those skilled in this art of intimacy, which photography would never cease to be, even if the community of iconoclasts grew prodigiously with the impatient offensive of a generation that had sophisticated this discipline on the market of snapshots-for-rent, a discipline formerly known only for its domestic uses.

Yet how can one measure simply – with a rigorous neutrality that doesn't preclude a certain fantasy – the long course of the most bumpkinish of urban photographers, when the figures – streaming out as if from a slot machine in Las Vegas (America) – propel Robert Doisneau, the joker and illustrious illustrator born in Gentilly (France), as much towards the pantheon of migratory birds already nesting on the Internet, as towards the artistic mutual funds column soon to be listed on the Stock Market?

IN THE PUBLIC DOMAIN

An example. In the summer of 1968, when Louis de Funès, directed by Jean Girault, was shooting *Le gendarme se marie [The gendarme gets married]*, Robert Doisneau calls to witness Moulins, capital of the department of Allier, for an entire month. Oh, it was next to nothing, just an amateur exhibition advertised through posters designed by a local art student in his Rameses II stage, complete with falcons, faulty perspectives and the forger's self-portrait (one thyroid eye as round as a flying saucer and a teeny-weeny body à la Giacometti). Not only did these photographs earn him praise from the local press, the ineradicable [and aptly named] fiefdom of Alexandre Vialette, *La Montagne*, but from the public as well. As the local curator Madame Fontseré would write him with pride in a letter dated 3 September 1968, with profuse excuses for having been so long in announcing the exciting news but here at last it is, dear friend, her colleagues being away on vacation and she on maternity leave very soon to give birth (she is quite specific on the point that, one would think oneself in a Fernand Raynaud comic sketch, "the birth has already failed to produce itself several times… "). The mother-to-be promised the imminent return of the photographs and then added in a postscript the number of visitors having had the privilege of admiring them: 1253…

Twenty-seven years later, the Robert Doisneau retrospective at the Musée Carnavalet, former letter-writing temple of the late Madame de Sévigné, will total, in the space of five months, 145,000 visitors – and this in spite of Alain Juppé's "Black December", paralyzing transportation strikes and the general grumbling of the winter of 1995… All of which would tend to prove that today Doisneau's name has fallen into the public arena as well as on to the artistic stage (did Valérie Lemercier not speak of a photograph "à la Doisneau" in her last one-woman show at the Théâtre de Paris?). Does this go so far as to imply that everyone has an idea, more or less, of what a Robert Doisneau photograph is, and what it is not? For, from among a public magnetically drawn to the Musée

Carnavalet, there were numerous viewers who came running armed with the faithful intention of pronouncing that "Paris-will-always-be-Paris" and who discovered, coincidentally, that there was a name, previously unknown to them, hiding behind the picture frames...

If, two years after his death, no one claims to know the answers to questions concerning a near future (who are the photographers who, in 2026, will impress students in the Multimedia division of the visual sciences?), it is nonetheless possible to venture two or three hypotheses about a certain Robert Doisneau and about this funny profession – photographer – which has become in such a short period a bubbling magic potion. "When I began making photographs, this profession was seen in the same light as the fellow who sells tinder stones in the subway, or ties at the bus stop. It was on the same rung of the social ladder. It was different. Today, they've even given me a medal. (...) In my time, no photographer was treated with this deference" (in *Les Inrockuptibles*, no. 18, 1989).

Much more than simply granting photographers a decent status, this Legion of Honour and this "retro-deference" indicate how great, even gigantic, is the gap between an art-fair-phenomenon Doisneau and a vintage Doisneau. Between a mistreated Doisneau and a booked-out Doisneau. Between a gobbled-up Doisneau and a nervously dissected Doisneau. Therein resides part of the mystery. There in that indivisible interval which would encompass a world war and undermine the fate of a whole class of good men, in that novel passage where a conscientious, sensitive kid transformed himself into a patented adept. It's a mystery that's tricky to solve, for in spite of the abundant material evidence left by Robert Doisneau, the key is still missing: his solitude. Solitude not in the sense of a self-imposed, hermetic regime, but in the sense of a corporal gymnastics, a happy, inexorable solitude in which one fights to move forward and confront the subject, no matter what its nature: good or evil.

A MEMORY LAPSE

Doisneau, a man confronting the metamorphoses that were acting on Paris, notably Les Halles, his village within the city. A witness to these changes, affected by the capitalist jolts, cursing, moaning, griping about politicians and their funereal entourage of paper-pushing bailiffs. An "inoffensive photographer seen as a gentle maniac" (1) trying to save the covered markets of Les Halles, attempting to fill in with a pickaxe a future memory lapse from which "technocrats high on geometry" were already hanging. This is what he writes: "The church of Saint-Eustache village is itself a blend of Gothic styles and smells, inside redolent with incense and celery, outside marked by a Renaissance feel and a strange humanity milling about in a carnivalesque light: the filthy rich and streetbums, truck drivers and pickpockets, butchers and fashionable clients of Dior, fish-sellers and drunks, and everyone addressing one another with a friendly familiarity. But most of all, there was a grand gaiety and happy goodwill hovering in the air, qualities which computers cannot register. This entire neighbourhood was petrified by a cruel freeze. Paris is losing her belly and some of her very soul. "

It's crazy how yesterday's past ends up looking like a once-upon-a-time present. Only yesterday, the painter Renoir was cursing electric lighting ("canned, bottled up and only useful for lighting up cadavers! "), while the holy candles of the Saint-Eustache church illuminated like a "shimmering fairy tale" the "deeply moving faith" of early Mass-goers: "the strong ones from Les Halles with their enormous hats in hand, slaughterhouse butchers with blood-stained aprons, oyster-shuckers in clogs and short petticoats, milkmaids dressed all in white. " From the elder Renoir, Doisneau learned that hidden in the faces and sweaty silhouettes of these worn out, humiliated people were the last of the Mohicans governed by a sixth sense: duty. And if he didn't exploit this living treasure shaped by genetic rivalries passed down from father to son, all in all it was thanks to him that this has been inscribed in the short history of the contemporary gaze.

Though blessed with a natural comic temperament and light-hearted wit in the tradition of *Tontons Flingeurs*, Doisneau did not appreciate "monstrous images made with an impatient desire to be original. " But what about him then? What was he like? Banal? Why banal when, on the contrary, he distinguished himself from common mortals, even if he took great care to pass unnoticed with his anonymous Michel Audiardesque physique. To fit the stereotype of a boy born at the dawn of the twentieth century, rather nondescript, emerging from a childhood clouded by the disappearance of his mother, further complicated by an absent father called off to the front. (One can still find this same kind of suffering today chatting with kids from the Third World, a pain that others have experienced before them, in families that have lost a mother or father so young, from illness, war, abortion... and they all whisper that same cruel word: "orphan".)

Educated at a university located in the forsaken desert surrounding Paris, in Gentilly (Val-de-Marne), Robert Doisneau honed his personality with a few breaststrokes in La Bièvre, a stream of "mucous" water, and trained himself to slip under the fence, to observe, aim and shoot, flexible as a piece of twine, that toy which is a child's reality. An agility which nurtured his aptitude for inventing stories that we ought to believe because they could be true and probably are. Such as his violin lessons at Kremlin-Bicêtre "in a building where two floors were reserved for music" and a keyhole intrigue between the violin teacher (pasty-faced Don Juan with a scar on his cheek) and the piano teacher (dazzling blonde). Or the reunion at the Terminus café with good ol' Marcel and Jean-François, when, with a merry toast, they decided to give it all up and take off at once, "three hilarious guys in a snazzy Peugeot, " hurling themselves like anti-Lascauxian buffalo toward the Southwest where they landed, after a thrilling slalom between the sycamores lining the road, smack dab in front of the "brand new Hôtel du Neveu. A wheelbarrow filled with geraniums, wash pan hanging from the wall and wagon wheel from the ceiling. We were in the flamboyant back country. "

THE FELLOW WITH THE VELVET CAP

If he amused himself by orchestrating new-born utopias or inciting sandcastle revolutions, principal activity of teen-agers gifted in practical tasks, Doisneau let reality trot along at its own pace, settling down in the last row in order to enjoy the show better later on. At first he was like a guest who wipes his feet before entering the privacy of his host's home, as much at ease among wealthy folk as proletarians, as comfortable with high-rolling jet-setters as knife-wielding bosses of the underworld. Lover of books and radio broadcasts. Weekend gardener. Smoker of *Gitanes* (filters). Creature of habit who could eat Chinese every noon and the very same dish when he wasn't even that crazy about it (and who, like so many men of his generation, was most likely incapable of boiling himself an egg and wouldn't have known the difference between the lavender-scented white handkerchiefs and the dishtowels piled up in the linen closet). He had only one cheque in his wallet but the unheard-of luxury of Westons on his feet and a velvet cap on his head, bearing the label of a famous hat-maker on the Place Vendôme, not the pig-Latin phrase printed on his cap from the Estienne School ("Noli altum saver sed time"), where he had to "succumb to four years of training from 1925 to 1929 to receive a diploma in lithographic engraving, with no real job opportunities in printing at the other end" (in *A l'imparfait de l'objectif*, Belfond). Those close to him point out how disarming was his simplicity and brilliant his kindness, or rather good humour (even on holidays, quite charming), how expressive his light-hearted manner of speech, sprinkled with a vocabulary as subtle and polished as a fine Muscadet. He was a man of the Parisian people whose lowliness and generosity he shared – someone who was never discouraging where he wasn't involved.

Those who care little about gaining his respect point to Doisneau's lack of authority – which he complained of himself – and the indecisions which allowed him to tolerate the reframing of his photographs: "I was used to being clipped down to size, working in square format; it never corresponded to the magazine layouts" (confession to Frank Horvat, in *Entre Vues*, Nathan Image). And to enduring, with no eyebrows raised, editorial rebuffs, which he wasn't taken in by anyway, the kindly prince having a strong aversion to narcissistic conflicts and guerrillas in three-piece suits. He had a penchant for destroying his own work with offhand remarks and for underestimating himself, with all the speed of a purge, in the wake of a malicious boomerang that he'd hurl out upon arrival in the afternoon at the Rapho Agency, where everyone, accountants, secretaries, typists, pined to hear more of his stories about a very ordinary existence: "Oh, I missed another great picture! "

And many respected him highly

And many respected his capacity for hard work and for becoming increasingly involved in writing – despite the difficulty this presented him with – which leaves us an indelible image of his poetic warmth. A friendly closeness with Jacques Prévert, pavement-pounding pal, while encouraging him in his quest for popular riches and the Lacanian musicality of common names, must also have complicated his task: a poet friend's art of expression might prove a pure joy, but it's a hard act to follow.

LIKE A RUSTY WEATHERVANE

It's important to try to evoke an image of Robert Doisneau even if it is slightly embellished or incomplete – after all, we're not the cops. Not because a good part of him would come through in his photographs, quantitatively (that's just claptrap, obviously he's in there, it's his eye), but because we detect, almost in spite of him, that arc stretched in perfect balance between his daily life and his photographs. This is really the most incredible aspect, and he always doubted it, really and truly, the poor misunderstood soul. It was enough to meet him once to sense all of a sudden the moment when he became as stiff as a rusty weathervane, as if by focusing on Paris and her peripheral sheath, this monolingual man had not chosen the right direction. As if he didn't have a place across from the Hungarian expatriates or those "pif-paf guys", the legendary reporters of *Life* magazine who ate up time zones like a mad cow and tamed, to all outward appearances, the laws of international gravity.

A winter memory. In 1989, while an exhibition at the Great Hall of the Villette Science Museum retraces the Renault years (1934-1939), Sebastião Salgado visits him at his home in Montrouge, where Doisneau had been living since

1937, leaving his car at the Jules Ferry plaza, not yet defiled by unsightly parking meters. Doisneau opens the door of the studio in a cloud of *eau de toilette* (he was very particular about his grooming), and they embrace with great shouts and thump each other on the back – "Hey, Robert, Hey, Sebastião" – delighted with this planned reunion. So that's the setting. What will they talk about? A load of nonsense.

About the Basque beret used as a shutter for wooden-chambered cameras. About blast-furnace number 6, out of commission in Dunkerque but performing better than number 2. About industrial wastelands. About the world's ugliest and least reliable car, lovingly manufactured in the Ukraine, in the city of Zaporojie. About quantum mechanics. About how astrophysicists are more reassuring than the local priest. About the photograph that is a photograph and yet nothing more than an artisan's craft of climactic and aesthetic variations. About film reserved for infallible souls. About the image of a chicken under a baobab tree snapped by the strange Edouard Boubat. About the Loire, a deceptively calm river, sly even, swallowed up in an apotheosis of châteaux and vineyards after rolling around in mountain snow. About soporific evening slide shows. About Monsieur Seguin's goat. About the Southern Cross…

And then, just before doubling over in laughter when Salgado starts in on his Brazilian genealogy and his boa-trapper father-in-law, Doisneau says: "Your walk through the world develops far more intelligence than spinning your wheels in Billancourt for five years. Always looking for a way to escape yourself, being all the while trapped by your pay cheque. Fortunately, they've come to a decision about me; I was finally sacked for always being late. They made a courageous choice where I'm concerned. But it's not easy to travel. Languages, jet lag, currencies, it all terrifies me. I remember a moment of anxiety in Canada, where I had just landed after a trip that was much too long for me. There I was in my bedroom like a package awaiting an unknown recipient. It was snowing outside, and I had the same feeling that I used to have at school when I was a boy. At four o'clock, I wanted only one thing: to go home, to go back to our house" (in *Libération*, 3 January 1989).

That "our house" echoes like a password. Or even a Rosebud. And it's precisely that "our house, " that mark of frightening, fairy-tale tenderness which certain attentive viewers catch today in Robert Doisneau's work. As if a hodge-podge life of negatives, of dozens of books, wheelbarrows full of postcards, tons of posters and television shows, had been necessary for that gay-tinged sadness to finally see the light of day, a sadness that permeated the world around which Robert Doisneau's no-frills, no-sweethearts merry-go-round revolved.

13

THE FEINTING MACHINE

Sunday, a day-off. Labourer Doisneau ignored the heavy wooden chamber and the glass plates stored in the film holder, removed it from its guaranteed – pure cast – iron tripod and presto, good riddance, space for the precious Rolleiflex. He left just like that, off on an adventure, sniffing the air in search of a trail. No net cast, no particular desire to catch an exotic beast – elephant, monkey, white whale – he just took off straight ahead. It was a peaceful pleasure, soccer fans and party revellers noisily giving vent to their feelings, threepenny shows and pink swirls of candyfloss for well-behaved children.

For us zombies, voluntarily stuck in air-conditioned booths with integral fax and elevator, this fresh-air mania seems bizarre, even if it's obvious that we ought to learn his Paris suburbs before the televised tragedy (or jogging, and, now with the Right's return to power, the bicycle, hell-on-wheels for pedestrians, this can only end badly). This changes the context of the "all-risks class" voyage that Doisneau undertook with his feinting machine, a much more useful apparatus than the time-clock which, after he "gave himself up to the Renault factories where 40,000 workers were detained, " would betray him by keeping track of his repeated tardiness…

A Rolleiflex break. During the Bardot & Scoobie Doo years, Doisneau bought a Leica, but the Rolleiflex – introduced in France in 1927 – was his little darling. The Leica, a lively and precise instrument which played an important role in the photo-journalistic revolution, was invented by a German, Oskar Barnack. He was an oddball from the high peaks, of fragile constitution to boot, who, having had enough of wandering about in the mountains with his camera sticking to him like a grizzly in heat, realized that it ought to be possible to reduce the whole thing to a Jivaro block on the principle "kleines Negativ, grosses Bild" ("small negative, large photograph"). Chosen by jockeys of the black and white scoop since its introduction on the market in 1924, the Leica is the teddy bear of big-time reporters; they adore it and swear only by it. But Doisneau opts for the atypical Rolleiflex: square negatives (6 x 6) and, in particular, a stomach-level viewfinder which leaves the photographer's face free (he doesn't have one eye stuck in the lens, his nose sticking out like a big cauliflower and his arms flapping in the air) and allows him to navigate with his camera like Amundsen with his compass.

For Doisneau, so openly shy, the Rollei is a crutch. It encourages his furtive side. He becomes a poser. And a pauser, for the Rolleiflex sends back an upside-down yet extremely sharp image. And through its lens he lives the striking hours, glued to the asphalt, a caged bird, ready to take flight…

What is it that he's doing, Robert Doisneau, standing dumbly on a street corner with his Rolleiflex that no one could mistake for a fishing pole, or at least for being hooked on "Perdu de vue" [read: TV trash]?

Nothing… he's watching… he's waiting.

What is he waiting for?

Why, a bite, of course! And… what a bite!

At the end of his line, a flower seller. A Mister Fixit dad. An idle cop. Newlyweds. A well-stacked streetwalker. Acrobats from the age of 7 to 77. A Mimile house. A massive stone stairway in the moonlight. A hideous scarecrow. All kinds of rare birds. Year-round merchants. Bronze statues. A crabby concierge… For sure, none of this has anything to do with what flows in the Vianon, the country stream trickling through the Corrèze, where he experienced his first trip with a line and felt with conviction that he had desecrated the divine, had interrupted the moving picture of time by reeling in a fish… He is six years old and he's got something going with the invisible, with the gooey monsters that prowl about and cackle in the night, watching over abandoned children in the hope of saving one of them, one at the very least, from the rushing current of neglect.

Does he realize that his tree-like position creates the effect of someone caught red-handed for vagabondage? Yes. Here's how he describes himself in 1991, in the preface of a book published in Japanese: "Daring to stand on a sidewalk and to remain motionless not for just a few seconds but for an hour or more, like a free-standing statue, you'll observe just how much this strange behaviour can attract the shipwrecked in the human sea. Singing the praises of immobility to one's contemporaries, who derive real pleasure from stepping on the accelerator pedal, comes close to being desperate provocation. If I dare to do this it's only because I seem to recall noticing a few of my posters on the walls of a luxurious duplex apartment where a dynamic young executive lived, fruits reaped from bygone days when curiosity and disobedience came to bloom. "

THE GRIP OF SUDDEN SENSATION

What's interesting about this preface, which he wrote in the last years of his life when he was "the oldest piece of furniture in the Rapho Agency, " is that he puts the whole parade on another level. One could say that he no longer embellishes the situation, that in fact, he rinses away its brilliant shine, effaces the romantic stamp that he emblazoned on everything he saw. All of a sudden a dull despair appears which no cheery jingle can dispel, along with the sense that he's going through an "apprenticeship for a future ghost" (as he would repeat at every possible opportunity). Soon it would be his turn to be meta-morphosed, to go through the ordeals that his subjects had already experien-ced: capture, development, exposure, appearance, display, confrontation, framing, disappearance… In a phrase: the grip of sudden sensation.

Doisneau did not mistreat his anonymous figures and hired models, even if there was a painful trial involving the couple who recognized themselves in the *Baiser de l'Hôtel de Ville* (and wanted to be compensated for their efforts at the time since Robert Doisneau himself had been so well rewarded by posterity). He had just reversed the course of the photographic process. Shaken up the sequence. Replaced the reels. With him, the characters of the drama became real people.

If we don't focus on the pan-cultural *classicos* (the poet Queneau, the artist Chaissac, the film-maker Welles) or of the great minds of science (Louis de Broglie to the blackboard!) whom he immortalized, whom did the fellow with the vel-vet hat aim his Rollei at?

Just people, friendly and mean, ugly, young, poorly dressed, ill-mannered, grimy, expert winos, aces of first-rate dilapidation, on – cloud-niners, lowly gut-tersnipes, midnight misfits, tight-fisted penny-pinchers and generous glad-hands, alley cats, wild-eyed hobos, clog-shod merchants and slipper-footed concierges, floozy gossips in tulle, sly dogs, feather-brained bimbos and noon-time hawks, mechanics-to-be… In short, just day-to-day people. Anyhow anybodies, all of those who had the dizzy fortune of being born beneath an infrared star (which excludes straight-away Claudia Schiffer, poor lass).

Ever since Prévert hypnotized him with his morsels of popular culture polished like diamonds in the rough, Doisneau collected in his net everything that trai-led along in the streets, everything that happened in the neighbourhood, eve-rything that disrupted the logical course of courses in leisure. He had the premonition – how else would one put it – to seize all that would become beau-tiful. Not what is beautiful; that nuance is important. From that sprang his infa-tuation with Les Halles, stinky, bloody, sweaty Les Halles, pig's heads and scalding vats, ugh! …

Earlier, in an equally original but more fine-feathered milieu, Jacques-Henri Lartigue had the same cocooning instinct for close-range photographs (as one might refer to a picture with local flavour). Lover of all that moved, of all that jumped, of all that lived.

And as Lartigue offered his relatives a view of the future through photos as lovingly crafted as a beautiful handwritten letter, Doisneau added the music, recording the lament of Madame Lulu, "useful singer": "You can't imagine how I love you / It's so sweet to be caressed."

Figurehead of the Doisneau style, Mademoiselle Anita. Her fresh, young, unattractive face belongs to a range of images taken in 1951 at the Boule Rouge in Paris, on that same rue de Lappe where Simenon chastely danced the Java (fifty centimetres apart from his partners!) before, as he complained, it became transformed into a reservation of tourists haunted by fake Apaches. It's a portrait taken after a request for authorization, the "May I take your picture, Sir? " so dear to swooner Salvatore Adamo. In his archives this photograph has been assigned number 28046. Doisneau calls it by name, Mademoiselle Anita, he knows nothing more than that; she was just a stranger he met in a cabaret whom he would never see again. But she reminds him of Polaire, snooty princess of the café-cabaret circuit with the waistline of a wasp (forty centimetres!) who, according to her rival Mistinguett, "approved of neither literature, nor drugs, nor any other dubious pleasures" and who was "furthermore, old-fashioned as soon as her corset freed her waist. "

In a 1990 episode of *Contact*, a television series devoted to photographers' contact sheets, Doisneau recounts for Sylvain Roumette the following spontaneous striptease: hearts up!

"All of a sudden, she offered to take off the little bolero that she wore. She appeared, shoulders bare, arms positioned very, very geometrically, just like this... Except for the hand, I would have liked the hand to be extended but in the end perfection is not of this world, thank god, and the picture remains human... Before taking off her bolero, she was more anonymous, I mean, there she was in her black clothes – but the arms are missing, there's an element missing here. Earlier, of course, before approaching her, I took a more general view of all of the young girls waiting for their suitors, their legs reflecting on the floor... Which seemed kind of pretty, all of those reflecting legs. It was really pretty. I was right... to wait and muster up the nerve to venture a 'May I? ', 'yes, ' and then on her own, she took off her little bolero. That's when the cocoon opened up and out came a butterfly. "

What is it that sticks out from this impromptu meeting with the French miss of the Boule Rouge, romantic heroine tinged with an air of sadness à la Françoise Sagan? That he worms his way into the decor like a slippery eel, like Garou-Garou with his mysterious walk-through-the-wall trick, even if he did manœuvre a bit before making out the old-fashioned brunette, slipping on the roller-skates of a weekend dauber, taking a pass across well-waxed floorboards where the little legs shone back. What is it then? The fact that she trusts him. And that this tacit agreement surpasses any coquetry implied by her stripping off the bolero; she could have tossed her hair or thrown out her chest. But no, she wisely lowers her eyes. In her heart, what is it that Anita wants? A suitor. Maybe a whole group of them. In any case, a masculine gaze. While Madame Lulu bellowed for a squeeze, Mademoiselle Anita would have her love song for free.

THIS ROUND'S ON ME

A stationary photographer is not protected from cannon balls, he can, in fact, find himself right in the line of fire. With Robert Giraud of the interminable Gauloise and "counter-top calluses", Maubert, Mouffetard and Les Halles being his favourite variety of this particular growth, Doisneau made the rounds of the midnight streets. Mademoiselle Anita was one of the sirens in this miraculous sea, a pearly dove fallen from the sky while he was waiting to hear Jeanne Chacun, a singer fallen into the flotsam of forgotten souls. There is nothing more typically Parisian than a bistro. There is nothing more French than a star-bottled litre of no-name red. There is nothing more elusive than those hot-tempered conversations, tongues wagging, necks unfurled, from which erupt, like babies' burps, bits of sentences as twisted as a highway cloverleaf. Doisneau regretted not being able to record these evening conversations in their context, but like certain of his colleagues, he was mindful of the other clients. Considerately acting as the interpreter of, indeed the accomplice to their silence. Not playing the party-pooper. Not firing a shotgun aimed right at their heads (Blaise Cendrars writes: "He takes his pick" which is absolutely true, but perhaps today, in view of the apprentice-paparazzi in temporary freedom, Cendrars would soften his jab of autumn 1955)…

He must have loved those tough owls, as he had loved Giraud, with his mouth loose enough to would make the Queen blush. Cendrars, the "roving rummy," taking great care to avoid the cocktail lounges, returning instead to Widow Moreau's place on the rue de l'Arbre-Sec, specialist in tonics and kidney-vetching spirits, to say nothing of menstrual potions reserved for department store salesgirls or, "rarer still and much more secret, an electuary for elderly gentlemen, medal-bearing or not, but in good health, one or the other of whom would always linger in the back room, making for a very awkward situation, and then slip away with his purchase: 'Saint-Antoine', elixirs, jars of aphrodisiacs to be warmed up in a pan of warm water" (in *Bourlinguer*).

"You're not one of those aperitif-drinking idiots, are you?" Paul Léautaud questioned him, worried at seeing Doisneau as thin as a bird despite his forty years (thus Léautaud's logical diagnosis of tuberculosis!).

"Do you want a glass of beer?" Picasso had asked at coffee-and-croissant hour, before being swallowed by the camera in his navy-striped shirt, his greasy, web-footed hands, those incredible four-fingered rolls baked in a brick oven by the bread man in Vallauris (R.D. reels off these two jokes to René Deroudille as Alain Vollerin mans the camera).

From these friendly drinks were born rather tender photographs, no insistence on the hang-overs, even if that universe was pretty far from having any relation whatsoever to the studio in Montrouge, where, lifeless, behind the scenes, the cardboard boxes of mischief started to pile up, floods of photographs estimated today at 400,000 negatives, more or less. In the bistros, those indeterminate places appropriate for all walks of life, workmen in overalls looking like red-nosed clowns and lazy bums subscribing to the *Canard Enchaîné* [satirical weekly newspaper], Doisneau must have felt at ease. Why? Because here there was nothing to do but watch, in this incessant, hectic bustle there was a new show to take in. It was paradoxically reassuring for him too, he who in the darkness saw not a void but a "threat of eternity," to borrow a phrase from Bachelard, philosopher-king. Through this interior landscape, turned in to focus on itself, Doisneau – who chasséed through Paris better than a veteran cabbie – waltzed along, well before the day of the Twingo (yes, yes, he did have his driver's license).

But he was above all an outdoor man.

He quivered with impatience. Blue sky outside. Sun. Light. Hop it! Get a move on! He's already far off…

Who was it who said "I march with the herd"? You win, it was Doisneau! And he ran off to one of those oases where Robinson Crusoe took refuge before his golden exile, to one of those neighbourhoods or Parisian passageways as bewitching and lightly populated as the canary cage of Paul Barabé, the actor-concierge at 46, place Jules-Ferry in Montrouge. The fellow who resisted the "Gestapo tornado" by smashing up the paper-forger in the cellar, a machine which could have taken on the shape of a portable guillotine… That was during the war.

THE HUMAN BEAST

In October of 1984, thinking about the feeling of joy that had forced him out of his studio and away from the commissions he had to fulfil (which often bored him), Doisneau points out that he never wanted "to leave future generations a testimony of Paris from the period when I was trying to get by." No, he borrows Paris at random, but with the instinct of a homing pigeon ("If they learned to read orientation maps, they would lose their sense of direction"). Immediately dismissing the districts with maids on every floor ("Locked out of these, I think of the ingenuous Baroness Haussmann who simpered: 'It's so strange, every time my husband buys a building, the demolition team arrives!'"), he stops in places that bear witness to man's suffering, places that I find laden with dignity, where the motions of life are performed with utter simplicity and the faces of those who arise early are very touching."

Smooth talk? It would be misleading to picture him as a mere slave weighed down by the sappy refrain of a blockbuster film. He likes humanity, even if, go figure why, in an act of ill-temper unworthy of an abstract sculptor unjustly accused during his trial for formalistic perversion, Constantin Brancusi – the grouch – had sneered: "You have the eyes of an assassin"... Even Robert Doisneau considered himself cruel for certain of his photographs, "Papa's airplane," for example, taken during a race of flower bedecked carts at Choisy-le-Roi, in 1934 – but with hindsight, if there was any ferocity in that picture at all, psst, guess what?!, it has since evaporated.

This simple sincerity towards humankind is systematically brought into doubt by those who prefer Willy Ronis one day (and his range of images of unequalled splendour), and Edouard Boubat the next (and his cosmic homeopathy for Duchampian bachelors), and nobody the next (it's Saturday and the critical critics' day off). These ticklish reproaches would tend to deprive him of his humble gaze, to demote him from the joyful gang of humanists – pretty dumb, isn't it? Yet it is precisely here that we find the protein-rich value of his photographic quest: the human race, seen as an optical illusion, constantly observed, stalked, disturbed, rearranged, in the hope of crushing on the spot – what crazy passion – that omnivorous chameleon capable of imitating all the world's mammals and of self-destructing in the blink of an eye, so the story goes...

He has his moods sometimes, Robert Doisneau, he's not a robot programmed for eternal delight (or bliss, even if he does read James Thurber, an American comic funny enough to make you fall off your seat, a caricaturist of the minimalist laugh variety). On some grumpy days, he sees double, hee hee hee, it's boiling inside his brain, it's burning rubber, watch out for falling blood pressure, then, bam!: "I see the mercantile conspiracy pouncing on everything needed to survive. Bottled water. Lighting. The racket surrounding parking spaces." This was his anguish at watching the old way of life disappear. And through clever marketing, it extended into his domain: cameras with integral flash convertible to microwaves will free the photographer from even the mere "effort of watching."

When he's in a good mood, it's a free-for-all, he's ready to leap, to develop his "personal little cinema" on demand. To bathe himself in sunlight, to purr like a cat on Colette's lap. A boldness aroused by night-time reveries, these nudge him off to pluck a dream still stuck in the good Lord's genuine duck-down pillow.

So let's follow him into the spell, ssh, don't make any noise, he's just got up (it's very early and everyone is still asleep, you'd take him for a sleepwalker). His pace is quick in the beginning, his limbs not yet awake, it's hard to open his eyes, but quickly quickly his body is carried along... And his eye lighting up, out of the blue, he moves into the city, into his city. Oh! how he needs the air, ah!, we can breathe in his photographs, we feel the air, he makes sure that they bathe in great draughts of it. And like a city ferret, he slides down the Chaussée d'Antin, an "aviary of pretty girls", then – head bowed, watch out! coming through! – he has an appointment of cap-i-tal-im-port-an-ce (as the Agency has told him again and again) in the garden district where advertising agencies bloom. Oops, he's late again, but there was that emergency picture to snap and how could he resist, it's not every day that he has this "rush of nerves" that lets him join in the conversation, lets him stare, laughing, at the clumsy youths in breeches clowning around. Doisneau can be heard saying to one of them: "Go on! bet you can do it again!"

It's quite surprising really, this complicity that Doisneau had with the *mise en scène*, a complicity that he didn't exploit, due, he said, to his lack of authority, but he had a sanctimonious admiration for the players. One August when he had stayed in Paris to work for Renaud, an urban singer, he related the follo-wing story to Sebastião Salgado: "One day, a young woman was running in the Montsouris park; all of sudden she fell down. As she seemed to be choking, a young man rushed over to revive her. He stretched her out on the lawn, then started by massaging her chest... Since she still wasn't coming to, he gave her mouth-to-mouth. Listen, Sebastião, here was this couple lying on the grass, it left all kinds of possible interpretations wide open. The suggestion of chance, it's crazy. I didn't take any pictures, it could have been embarrassing for them. You see, Salgado, that's what photography is, it's a zig-zagging gait..." This trivial incident is useful in showing that Doisneau wasn't necessarily spying. That he also possessed an innate passion for sheer illusion, for pure chimera, and that he needed to consume his personal supply of these like a vampire on a macro-biotic diet restoring his strength, eating in the glow of the fireside. Right, okay, there were two Doisneaus: the one who installed his mole – hole device, crou-ching behind the window of the Romi gallery with its naughty painting that scandalized turban coiffed housewives; and the other who, tired from dragging his feet around, allowed time the time to run its course, like an hourglass, and as for the chameleon's life, *basta*, enough is enough…

A GRAIN-FED SOCIOLOGIST

Three or four words about colour which also relate to time – magic, magic. When he left on assignment for Datar (in 1984, with a group of surveyors) at the request of François Hers and Bernard Latarjet, Doisneau decided to photograph the suburbs in colour, those suburbs that he detested as a child, too filthy, too ugly and less seedy than one might guess. These modern images are difficult for us to decipher for they do not benefit, so to speak, from a "past/present" mark. It's hard to get used to this sea of hideousness, but one sees in it, quite clearly, that Doisneau not only mastered the technique (framing and all that), but that he also had a point of view, just like that of a grain-fed sociologist, regarding the labourers' prefab housing, a sort of horizontal bar code parallel to the sky. Regarding the dissolution of earth-bound emotions deeply rooted in the soil (hence, curiously, many photographs shot vertically). And, in the end, pshaw!, we don't even give this a thought… As if in his readiness to trap anything and everything, he had become a flighty hunter aiming at everything that flew past his sights (right, it is also true that at times he overdid the Jacques Tati street-urchin routine, like a poorly directed actor of a box-office flop). No, no, on the contrary, Doisneau knows his world; no one enters his black box without his permission.

The proof: an excerpt from an interview with Rosi Huhn, on 26 February 1992 in Montrouge, when, with an air of confidence, he yields some ground on his light-sensitive surface: "Even politically, if one chooses to photograph people who work, and therefore suffer, it's already a choice, even if it's not stated in a philosophical manner. Generosity, for example, the ability to get inside other people's skin, that's what is important. The ability to espouse people's attitudes, it's a kind of mime in which one can easily recreate the gestures. And also knowing what it is to be cold or to have nothing to eat, that conditions you in your choice of subject matter (…). It's good to retain a kind of brotherhood… (…). It's simply because one is sensitive oneself. And then, you start to take pity on yourself; you'll complain a lot, 'poor old me, oh me oh my.' That counts too. I find myself in the position of the poor chap who doesn't understand anything, who is defenseless. The Clown! A character. To me it's more the tragic Clown than it is Jesus Christ. The poor fellow who is very fearful, who is without defense" (interview published in *Passages. (D') après Walter Benjamin*).

Reference to the Clown, rather to Monsieur Hulot whose bicycle he deconstructed with clinical precision, a grunge happening. And through the Presidents, flag-bearers of the Republic, Doisneau gained public and institutional recognition, he who had begun his career nabbing magnesium shots of suppositories and blisters (for pharmaceutical advertising, before being hired by Renault), it was an eccentric gaiety…

DOWN WITH THE PICTORIALISTS!

If Doisneau never failed to cite the name of André Vigneau, for whom he worked as assistant, it is, in part, evidence of his loyalty. It is also because his first boss, a sculptor converted to the fine art of imitation, had shown him the stark nakedness of photography: for his very own eyes. We have seen and seen again a certain rain-slicked street, trees reflecting in the asphalt… [a mile-stone photograph by André Vigneau which Doisneau would refer to repeatedly]. It is a brilliant reproduction from the '30s, a period teeming with shadow-eaters ever since the emigration of a group of Hungarian gurus to Paris: André Kertesz, Brassaï and the others would participate in dislodging the city from her lights and from her academic reserve. And would guillotine the pictorialist fat cats who never failed to drown their custom-tailored portraits in fog and stormy skies.

Flash-back. Sailboats moving along the Seine. Children placing bets in the gutter, wearing little sandals woven in Biarritz. It was a time when one still extended credit to good people, or to supposedly good people. Then the war broke out. Just when Doisneau, driven from Renault, could have given himself over to a few of his passions. In a way, it's as if the war that he lived as a loser, so he said, in contrast to the war fought by those in the Resistance (but he fought back, too, by forging documents), is buried beneath his photographs. Not the war of blood and corpses, wounds and barricades, albeit very photogenic according to him, but the equation of war = off-limits territory = land of privation = enclosure = duty = guilt. This does not necessarily mean that his photographs translate only as images of a field of honor with a "cemetery in Normandy" feel. Yet there is also a bit of that in him: a feeling of enclosure, of claustrophobia, of something that cannot be chased away. No, deeper than a melancholic sigh. Black thoughts? No doubt, but perhaps it's also about the gap between what he looks at and what he sees, between what he catches and what he keeps, between what he's seen and what he'll never see again. Always in a state of surprise. And Doisneau to set it right, to blow in some air, to patch up the tragedy of the real, a dynamic understudy for these scheduled disappearances.

It's ridiculous how quickly time flies. Yet even if photographers are no more conscious of it than others (they are perhaps all the more aware since they live off it; nostalgia is a bread-winner, sometimes even an income), it makes them nervous, this race against the clock. This race against death. Hence their urgency to freeze the living. The beautiful. The living and the beautiful.

Paris was no more beautiful in 1938 than it will be in 1998 or in 2056. But intermittently there is an ephemeral harmony between the living and the beautiful, and this is what Doisneau lifted on to his film. Between humans and human-thinking machines. Between trees and skyscrapers. A eurhythmic well-being in which the poor coexisted with the not-so-poor and with the rich who didn't overly pride themselves on being over-fed. Households of frizzy hair and fashion models eating their fill. Bleached blonde barmaids and leukaemic hoodlums, ever mindful of their offspring in tow. It's an ideal of humanity devoid of the Benetton cynicism that strikes us today; it's like leafing through an old, ink-stained schoolbook, as if it were inscribed in our personal history. So what if Robert Doisneau saw the world the wrong way around, against the flow, while his neighbours nibbling at English bait hurried off to America to strike it rich? So what if he wove lucky charms from real life, from a fatally unrepeatable past? It might have been a past that was anything but exemplary but it certainly was beautiful, dramatically beautiful.

EYE OF THE NATION

Prize pupil of the State? Clichéd paragon? Ah yes, we inevitably come to that tear-jerking question where we reach for our hankies. The teary traffic in sentiment, sappy drivel, ho hum…

Yeah, well, to tell the truth, time floating slowly by like the barge *Arletty* on the Saint-Martin canal was to Robert Doisneau's advantage. He managed to make ends meet, got old, played hard at being Robert Doisneau, prize pupil of the French State. He seemed to take pleasure in it, sometimes. We got tired of it, often… Were we wrong, and he right, or the other way around? Wrong question. Certainly, success is just eyewash, but unsuccess…

Look at Eugène Atget… It's fashionable nowadays to associate the two of them… Eugène Atget, the failed thespian, retrained as a Montparnassian with nary a nickel, slaving away so humbly, what a drag, and now today, his papers stamped SAMS (sublime absolute must-sees), worth a pretty penny. And the other, Robert Doisneau with his newsboy cap, crony of primitive Paris, artisan of the dangerous streets where the piss of pastureless horses on the Butte-Montmarte ran down the gutters in streams. They both had a passion – unquestionable and actively pursued – for the street, for the public plaza, for the movie cinema strip. For passageways that led benevolent predators from one astonishment to the next, from one shop to another, from one love to another… The field of action of these two visionaries, less corny than they might appear (for the latter at least) : Paris and her secret labyrinth, Paris away from the crowd, the essence of bottled Paris.

The Atget vintage (1857-1927)? So much is already known. And Doisneau?

We can predict that his public success will continue to grow, or at least, that our beloved public will not retract its favour: postcards, pillow slips, posters, calendars, appointment books, yes, it's all there for the buying.

Will we discover, later on, another Doisneau, a neglected Doisneau, an unknown Doisneau? We can't be sure, given that when alive he was already a gold mine to those who, near or far, hoped to meet him. But the day will come when a few less sugary antidotes will be recovered contesting the proof, chalked up as immortal; yoo-hoo! just like that, not to be a bother, just raising a finger of doubt…

Then we'll see that he knew certain sorrows, this lover of fleeting beauty, this confidante of happy days, we'll see that sometimes he would hire actors to box it up once and for all…

Then we'll read a few excerpts from his spiral notebooks:

"Paris is touching because threatened, temporary, ephemeral. "

"The intellectual has his photographer like the Marxist has his priest. "

"Lack of respect is disappearing. To photograph is to disobey. It's to be attentive to values that are scorned. It's not about keeping track of the stock market index. It's about bringing into question. It's about not giving a damn. Hold on to your green plants and your golden thrones. "

"We must demonstrate through our general attitude that we have at our disposal a ready supply of generous interest which under no circumstances should be confused with a kind of brusque customs search. So that in theory, the meeting, the encounter, will cease to bear that sporty sense which connotes the collision of two adversaries. "

"The image is much better suited to suggest than to describe. "

"Let us defend the [French] Republic. "

"Already… Oh, I have to go home already. It's dark. "

And someone will turn on the light.

ARM IN ARM

Trafficking in the unreality of the real, Robert Doisneau laid down the imaginary as a satisfying rule of thumb in the continual comings and goings of his life on earth, like a boarding-school student taking off right in the middle of a Vigo film to give his grandmother a kiss. A flick of the finger and there you are, one more photo in the black box. One too many? No one is forcing anyone to throw Robert Doisneau a life-jacket. Everyone has the right to hold a different favourite close to his heart, which is not exactly complicated given the host of photographers circulating beneath the so-called humanist horizon: Izis (with his shots as light as confetti), Marcel Bovis, Sabine Weiss (who had him hired by *Vogue*, grotto of freely available elegance), etc. All of them stitched a tapestry in which emotion preempts artistic subject – matter out of hand, though one would be hard pressed to detect in their vision the scent of a patriotic password.

But they have common fascinations – the circus, artists, lovers – strolls that they seem to have taken arm in arm, and share the desire to photograph locals with a carelessness that is not always faked. Each reserves at the end of the roll the right to have his say, which it would be pointless, of course, to underestimate, since comparisons only serve to fatten up polling institutes which are already terribly satisfied with their obese percentages.

What seems remarkable about Robert Doisneau is that he had this talent for condensing an anecdote into a spark as intense as an electrical current, like one of those bolts of lightning that bring about a sudden rainbow in a memorized landscape. A sort of inevitable, dazzling, fleeting apparition, with no reason for being, and destined, in theory, to dissolve once seen. Yet far from becoming a negative characteristic, Doisneau is enriched by its secondary effects... By his steadfast escape from reality. If he was going to tinker with it, he might as well try to make it last longer, like the undeveloped reel of the Buttes-Chaumont park that we play back in a continuous loop until our thirst is sated. By his determination to flee the situation of a stock photographer (obliged as he is to produce and they ask him to produce). By his fears about being human, completely silly, confronting the void. Which he filled with faces and more faces and more faces...

FALSE TRUTHS

Can one state, without lying, that Doisneau's work is a fireworks display, a sort of photo-album prefabricated by a public craze and therefore suspect of being pure schmaltz of dubious taste?

A cocktail-drinking moron would answer yes, thinking it might earn him a second swig of slosh at no extra cost… bottoms up, that one's solved, pigeon-holed life, next… A moron's opposite, one of that endangered species, would answer that artifice, already the engine of reality, has been inscribed in the medium of photography ever since its invention during the last century, long before cinematography, the art of motion. That there is nothing more misleading than a photograph and so, since we're showered with thousands of them every day, there is nothing more true…

Robert Doisneau's photographic testament is just a series of false truths most of which have legitimately become motifs used to weave into colorless conversations, to elicit and share the pleasure. When Doisneau would make a portrait of someone – a posed portrait – he had this way of acting the dummy. As if he wasn't going to be able to make it work, as if he wasn't aware of what he was doing with his crummy camera which didn't ever seem to be functioning properly, tcha, damn machine… He was a clever devil. A really clever one. As Jean-Claude Carrière explains, in the 6 December 1986 issue of *Jours de France*: "Little by little, you get into the game, you want to help him, you do all you can. You're even prepared to make a suggestion. And then, all of a sudden, when you start getting desperate, something lights up in his eye and he says: 'Ah! There, that's not bad.' Then, you feel happy for him because he seems to have overcome his difficulties. He still insists a bit, 'just to see.' You have the impression that for the price of an unheard of stroke of luck, he might just have gotten a picture, finally. (…) Doisneau's art was above all to make you forget that it was one."

And in his role of the foil, Robert Doisneau secretly stole the blackbirds' shiny tin and replaced it with his own captivating mirror… one whose presence is neither seen nor known.

(Those citations whose source is not given were taken from unassigned documents in Robert Doisneau's archives and, in some cases, from his spiral notebooks where he jotted down his inspirations.)

THE WAR

Previous page: Bicycle-taxi, Place de l'Opéra, 1942

32

Salting at Saint-Germain-des-Prés, 1942

Intersection at Saint-Germain-des-Prés, circa 1944

The Champs-Elysées, 1944

Rue de Castiglione, 1943

36

Butcher's shop, circa 1944

Line in front of a grocery, 1945

38

Shortage, circa 1944

Grocery, 1944

In the metro, 1945

Les Halles metro station, circa 1945

42

Monique Foucault's First Holy Communion in the basement of 46 place Jules-Ferry, Montrouge, 1943

Lamarck metro station during an air raid warning, 1943

Paul Barabé in 1945. Concierge of the building where Doisneau lived at the Place Jules-Ferry in Montrouge, he was from 1942 until his death in 1983 Doisneau's assistant and confidant

Champ de Mars, 1944

In a square, 1944

48

Market gardening in the Tuileries Gardens, 1944

The Beaubourg plaza, August 1944

50

Rue de Rennes, July 1944

Firewood supply, circa 1944

Outdoor beauty parlor, 1943

On the Champs-Elysées, circa 1944

Barricade at Ménilmontant, August 1944

Barricade on Boulevard Saint-Michel, August 1944

Barricade at the Place Saint-Michel, August 1944

Barricade at Ménilmontant, August 1944

Barricade at the Place du Petit-Pont, August 1944

60

Barricade, August 1944

Right: Place Saint-Michel, August 1944

62

After the ransacking of the Parti Populaire Français, Rue des Pyramides, 1944

Place de la Concorde, August 1944

64

Above and right: Rue de Rivoli, 1945

66

Place de la Concorde, August 1944

August 1944

68

Place de l'Opéra, 1945

Bicycle-taxi, circa 1944

TRAFFIC

Quai de Grenelle, August 1949

La Chapelle metro station, January 1953

75

On the Canal Saint-Denis, 1954

Bassin de la Villette, 1954

77

Canal Saint-Denis, 1969

Metro conductor, July 1955

At the bus depot, July 1955

Chambre des Députés bus stop, 1946

Boulevard Montmartre, May 1961

82

The number 38 bus, June 1959

Place de la Concorde, March 1950

Rue Royale, 1949

Above and right: Rue Tronchet, October 1954

88

Boulevard Montmartre, May 1961

Rue Saint-Antoine, May 1953

Intersection at Buci, 1947

The Champs-Elysées, 1946

The Beaubourg plaza, 1946

94

Quai de New York, March 1961

Quai du Louvre, in front of the Pont-des-Arts, January 1951

Invalides, July 1955

Place de la Concorde, circa 1938

April 1953

Rue de Seine, July 1955

Right: Bicycle-taxi, rue Saint-Dominique, July 1982

Go-cart, 1946

Place du Marché Saint-Honoré, 1950

On the quais, 1957

The Marquis de Cuevas' dogs, 1953

Above and right: Porte d'Orléans, 1953

Place de la Concorde, April 1949

Rue de la Paix, January 1951

Left: Place de la Madeleine, 1951

112

Place de la Madeleine, 1951

Place de l'Opéra, 30 May 1959

The Grands Boulevards, May 1955

Left: Boulevard Haussmann, April 1953

On the Champs-Elysées, 1946

March 1954

Boulevard Saint-Denis, May 1951

120

March 1950

Place de la Concorde, 1969

Place de l'Opéra, 1956

Left: Rue de Richelieu, October 1971

Rue de Rivoli, April 1953

Pont-des-Arts, June 1966

128

Place de la Concorde, 13 July 1971

Place de la Concorde, September 1969

130

Rue de Rivoli, 1978

Place du Carrousel, 1981

Gare du Nord, October 1971

134

Cour de Rome, October 1971

May 1965

Opéra metro station, 1961

138

On the train to Sceaux, 1946

PARIS AT
WORK

Previous page: Café Gervais, at 50 Rue de Rivoli, 1957

Monsieur Constant, café proprietor, Rue de Seine, December 1951

144

Delivery men of the daily communist newspaper « Ce Soir, » 1947

145

Rue de la Saïda, July 1972

In front of the entrance to the Renault factory, Place Nationale in Boulogne-Billancourt, 1945

148

The Champs-Elysées, November 1959

Palais-Royal, August 1955

April 1951

Rue du Four, September 1969

152

Rue Saint-Louis-en-l'Île, 1949

In front of the Luxembourg Gardens, 1953

154

The Champs-Elysées, March 1961

The Champs-Elysées, July 1951

Gas factory, Saint-Denis, 1955

158

Wash-house, Rue des Partants, March 1953

Canteen at the Renault factories, 1950

Above and left: The Renault factories, 1945

The Renault factories, Boulogne-Billancourt, 1950

Right: End of the day at the Renault factory, 1945

Tuileries Gardens, 1948

Quai des Tuileries, 1945

Place de Bitche, 1954

Champ de Mars, August 1950

Place de la Concorde, 1961

August 1955

March 1955

Rue de la Tombe-Issoire, October 1953

Quai de Bourbon, September 1967

Pont des Arts, June 1966

Pont des Arts, October 1950

Avenue de Breteuil, July 1955

Above and right: The Champs-Elysées, 17 May 1955

180

The Champs-Elysées, 17 May 1955

Right: Medici Fountain, Luxembourg Gardens, October 1950

Palais-Royal, June 1950

183

The Champs-Elysées, July 1959

Place de l'Opéra, 1955

Workmen's lunch, 1953

Concierge's lodgings in the 1st arrondissement, 1945

188

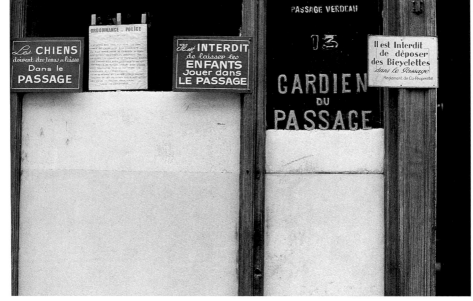

Passage Verdeau, January 1976

Right: Concierge, Rue Jacob, 1948

Madame Augustin, concierge on Rue Piat, April 1953

191

Concierge, 1948

67, Boulevard Barbès, 1938

National Lottery kiosk, Rue de Rivoli, 1948

National Lottery kiosk, April 1953

On the Grands Boulevards, January 1964

Flower market, 1946

198

Artisans' courtyard, 1945

Île Saint-Louis, June 1949

Undertakers, prison nursing home in Nanterre, 1952

Paul Arzens' car, 1951

202

October 1959

Rue du Faubourg Saint-Antoine, 1970

204

Jardin des Plantes, 1943

Rue du Département, 1952

Rue Raymond Losserand, October 1966

Courtine Fils, Rue Mouffetard, September 1981

Rue de la Tombe-Issoire, 1965

210

1945

Maurice Duval, rag-picker, watercolourist, 1947

212

Rue Mouffetard, April 1951

214

Rue de Grenelle, 1949

217

Rue Saint-Roch, 1965

Left: Rue Pixérécourt, February 1974

218

Rue Perrault, 1967

Passage du Caire, January 1976

220

Pierre Poilâne, December 1966

221

Eisenhower's visit to Paris in 1959

Place du Marché Saint-Honoré, 1945

224

Selling French fries, 1946

Selling roasted chestnuts, 1959

226

Lavender seller, December 1954

Rue des Lavandières-Sainte-Opportune, 1946

At the hairdresser's, 1946

Madame Huguette, Nougat Queen, 1953

At Bébert's, November 1959

232

VER
SOLITAIRE
Remède Unique
PAS
D'INSUCCÈS

La PHARM
est fourni
des ASSUR
SOCIAl

Front window of a pharmacy, 1932

At the corner of Boulevard Haussmann and Rue de Mogador, 1951

234

Above and right: Al Cabrol, wrestling champion, seller of lighters and flint stones, 1956

Above and right: Al Cabrol, wrestling champion, seller of lighters and flint stones, 1956

« Aerial Photography, » 1950

240

March 1958

241

March 1958

242

March 1955

Place de la Bastille, May Day, 1949

244

February 1960

Rue du Faubourg Montmarte, May 1961

Georges and Riton, rue Watt, 1952

Street singer, November 1952

Passage de la Trinité, 1952

Rue Saint-Denis, February 1953

Left: Les Halles district, circa 1946

Above and right: « Chez Nénette, » 1952

Colette at the Palais-Royal, 1951

Georges Braque in his Paris studio, 1953

Georges Braque in his garden in the 14th arrondissement, 1953

Paul Léautaud at Fontenay-aux-Roses, 1947

Jean Dubuffet, 1951

Alberto Giacometti in his studio, 46 Rue Hippolyte Maindron, 19 December 1957

Blaise Cendrars, 1945

Maurice Duval, watercolourist, 1949

César, 1955

Françoise Sagan, May 1956

Jean Tinguely at Trocadéro, 1959

Fernand Léger in his studio at Gif-dur-Yvette, 1954

LES HALLES

Previous page: View from the fourth story of Rue des Halles, January 1969

The last morning of Les Halles market, March 1969

272

November 1967

December 1952

November 1967

August 1967

November 1968

October 1967

278

December 1968

279

280

December 1967

Butchers' scalding vats on Rue Sauval, January 1968

November 1956

284

November 1956

Mr. Cartalade's café, Rue des Halles, February 1957

287

288

November 1959

November 1959

290

291

Le carreau des Halles, 1945

294

Rue de Rivoli, March 1955

March 1955

Les Halles through a telephoto lens, May 1953

After the market, September 1967

The demolition of Les Halles, September 1971

People looking into the pit of Les Halles, February 1975

The worksite at Les Halles, September 1976

Previous pages: The pit of Les Halles, November 1973

The worksite at Les Halles, September 1976

307

Opening of the Forum des Halles, 5 September 1979

Above and right: Opening of the Forum des Halles, 5 September 1979

MARKETS

Rue de la Chaussée d'Antin, April 1969

314

Rue Rambuteau, 1946

315

Place du Marché-Saint-Honoré, 1946

316

Jerusalem artichokes merchant, circa 1942

Circa 1938

318

Rue Mabillon, 1950

Rue de Seine, 1947

320

Rue Mouffetard, April 1951

Ménilmontant, March 1953

Les Halles, October 1964

Left: Rue Lepic, June 1969

Rue Mouffetard, April 1951

Madame Vivin, dancer at the Concert Mayol, Faubourg Saint-Martin, 1953

Rue Mouffetard, April 1951

327

Above and right: Rue Mouffetard, May 1951

330

March 1954

Rue Mouffetard, May 1951

Rue Mouffetard, 1945

Rue Mouffetard, April 1951

SUNDAY

Place du Marché-Saint-Honoré, 1946

Place du Marché-Saint-Honoré, 1945

Rue Auguste-Comte, 1932

340

Rue Pajol, 1953

In the 12th arrondissement, 1953

342

Boulevard Richard-Lenoir, October 1959

343

Rue Saint-Louis-en-l'Île, juin 1949

Rue des Canettes, Bastille Day, 14 July 1949

346

Rue Letellier, circa 1939

Quai de Jemmapes, June 1966

Rue des Canettes, Bastille Day, 14 July 1949

349

Rue des Couronnes, March 1953

Rue Saint-Louis-en-L'Île, June 1949

351

Rue des Canettes, Bastille Day, 14 July 1949

352

Above and right: Rue des Canettes, Bastille Day, 14 July 1949

354

Rue du Terrage, Bastille Day, 14 July 1951

Rue Robert Blache, Bastille Day, 14 July 1951

« Danse à la fontaine, » 1947 (Dancing at the fountain)

Above and right: Rue de Nantes, Bastille Day, 14 July 1955

360

Bastille Day, 14 July 1959

361

Rue des Canettes, Bastille Day, 14 July 1949

362

Rue Saint-Louis-en-L'Île, Bastille Day, 14 July 1949

363

Rue des Canettes, Bastille Day, 14 July 1949

364

Rue Saint-Louis-en-L'Île, Bastille Day, 14 July 1959

365

Bastille Day, 14 July 1959

367

Saint-Germain-des-Prés, 1947

Above and right: Saint-Germain-des-Prés, 1947

Saint-Germain-des-Prés, 1947

Saint-Germain-des-Prés, 1951

Above the Pont-Neuf, September 1956

The Genie of Bastille, May 1960

374

Le Moulin à Poivre, Boulevard de Clichy, December 1966

American tourists in a café, October 1958

Mademoiselle Wanda, street fair, Boulevard Saint-Jacques, 1953

The Café Curieux, circa 1965

380

Montrouge, 1945

381

La Java, November 1951

At the Quatre Sergents de la Rochelle, Rue Clovis, 1950

Mademoiselle Anita, La Boule Rouge, Rue de Lappe, 1951

Left: Mouffetard, November 1952

386

Saint-Germain-des-Prés, February 1950

387

Saint-Germain-des-Prés, January 1950

La Maison du Café, 1946

Above and right: Brasserie Lipp, 1947

392

Café de la Paix, May 1956

393

« Le Baiser de l'Hôtel de Ville, » March 1950

The dogs of La Chapelle, 1953

Jacques Prévert on the Quai Saint-Bernard, 1955

398

Marguerite Duras, Rue Saint-Benoît, February 1955

Fernand Léger in the Montparnasse district, 1946

Alberto Giacometti in a café in the 14th arrondissement, January 1958

Simone de Beauvoir at the Deux Magots, 1944

Orson Welles at the « Chasseur, » 1949

Jardin des Plantes, May 1951

The Champs-Elysées, 1946

Jardin des Plantes, 1953

26 February 1956

Winter 1945

410

Above and right: Montmartre, February 1958

412

Ménilmontant, May 1956

Ménilmontant, 1956

414

Place Saint-Sulpice, 1946

Rue Vilin, 1969

416

Ménilmontant, 1935

Belleville, 1969

Above and right: Montmartre, February 1953

On the outer boulevards, 1934

422

Tuileries Gardens, 1944

Luxembourg Gardens, March 1950

Champ de Mars, 1943

Left: Champ de Mars, june 1969

426

Under the Eiffel Tower, 1946

427

Photographer Yoshi Takata, December 1964

On the towers of Notre-Dame, June 1952

Trocadéro, March 1958

431

Tuileries Gardens, 1934

432

Above and left: Gardens of the Palais-Royal, June 1950

434

435

Tuileries Gardens, July 1951

Luxembourg Gardens, July 1951

AT THE
WATER'S EDGE

Booksellers' stalls on the banks of the Seine, 1947

442

Booksellers on the banks of the Seine, 1951

Monsieur Flinois, bookseller, January 1951

444

Bookseller on the Quai Saint-Michel, January 1951

Bookseller, January 1951

446

Pont-des-Arts, 1953

Pont-des-Arts, 1950

Île des Cygnes, October 1972

Pont-des-Arts, June 1966

On the quais, 1934

Quai de la Tournelle, March 1953

454

Quai de l'Horloge, July 1966

Near the Pont-Neuf, February 1951

456

457

Pont d'Iéna, 1945

Square du Vert-Galant, July 1947

Quai Henry IV, 1949

462

The banks of the Seine, June 1953

463

Rue des Deux-Ponts, 1953

466

Monsieur Dassonville and his duck, 1949

Place Saint-Michel, 1945

Fly fisherman, 1951

469

From the Pont-des-Arts, 1947

March 1950

Quai de L'Hôtel de Ville, 1946

Above and right: Fishermen on the banks of the Seine, 1951

476

Near the Pont Mirabeau, 1932

Canal Saint-Martin, 1953

Bassin de la Villette, March 1953

480

Quai de l'Oise, 1945

June 1955

482

Canal Saint-Martin, June 1953

Jemmapes lock, Canal Saint-Martin, March 1969

484

Bassin de la Villette, March 1957

485

Bassin de la Villette, February 1957

SHOP WINDOWS
AND
PASSAGEWAYS

Previous page: Romi, gallerist and collector, in front of his shop on the Rue de Seine in 1947, with Robert Giraud, author of *Vin des rues*

The front window of the Romi Gallery at 21 Rue de Seine, 1947

490

Above and right: The front window of the Romi Gallery at 21 Rue de Seine, 1947

492

Above and right: The front window of the Romi Gallery at 21 Rue de Seine, 1947

494

Above and right: The front window of the Romi Gallery at 21 Rue de Seine, 1947

Jacques Prévert, Avenue du Général-Leclerc, 1955

498

In front of Galeries Lafayette, February 1973

Georges Simenon, 1962

Passage des Princes, January 1976

502

Passage Jouffroy, March 1976

Passage du Grand-Cerf, February 1976

504

Dog on wheels, 1977

Passage Jouffroy, December 1980

506

Mr. Robert Capia, Galerie Véro-Dodat, January 1976

507

Passage Jouffroy, March 1976

Passage des Princes, January 1976

509

Passage Jouffroy, January 1976

510

The Vullin Bookshop in the Passage Jouffroy, December 1980

Passage Jouffroy, January 1976

512

Passage Véro-Dodat, February 1976

513

Passage du Prado, November 1951

514

Galerie Saint-Lazare, February 1976

515

Madame Léa, Passage du Prado, July 1980

Entrance to the Passage Jouffroy, January 1976

Galerie Vivienne, June 1980

A JOURNEY THROUGH PARIS

La cour des artisans, 1953

Rue Tholozé, 1935

Montmartre, circa 1934

At the corner of Rue Beauregard and Rue de Cléry, circa 1943

Winter 1944

Rue des Ursins, circa 1945

Quai de Montebello, circa 1947

528

Place Vendôme, 1948

Place Vendôme, winter 1946

530

Saint-Germain-des-Prés, 1945

531

Rue Levert, March 1953

Rue Vilin, 195

534

e des Partants, 1953

Montmartre, February 1958

Rue Broca

538

Above and right: Rue Broca, June 1964

540

passe Langlois, 15 February 1958

Bellevi^{ll}

Left: S⁻

544

Choisy, February 1975

Rue des Rigoles, 19

Left: Quai de la Rapée, Ma\

...dippolyte Church, Avenue de Choisy, March 1975. Right: Interchange at the Porte de Bagnolet, December 1975

550

Gare de Lyon, April 1975

Quai André Citroën, September 1977

La Défense complex, February 1975

La Défense complex seen from the rooftop terrace of the Esso Tower, September 1970

SUBURB

Issy-les-Moulineaux, 1947

Railway bridge at Villeneuve-Saint-Georges, 1945

The switchyard at Villeneuve-Saint-Georges, 1945

560

Saint-Denis, 1945

Saint-Denis, 1949

562

Sand quarries at Choisy-le-Roi, 1945

563

The Seine near Alfortville, 1945

Canal Saint-Denis, 1945

Coal collection, Saint-Denis, 1945

Alfortville, 1946

Cachan seen from the aqueduct, 1946

569

Avenue Président-Wilson in Saint-Denis, 1949

570

Arcueil, 1946

Issy-les-Moulineaux, 1945

572

Near La Courneuve, 1945

Saint-Denis, 1944

574

In the shantytowns, 1946

575

Ivry, 1946

576

Villejuif, 1946

577

La Bièvre at Gentilly, 1945

Villejuif, 1946

The « Plain » at Saint-Denis, 1944

581

Saint-Denis, 1946

Above and right: Near the Porte d'Ivry, 1945

584

Nanterre, 1945

585

Porte d'Italie, 1945

Josette's twentieth birthday, Gentilly, June 1947

588

Vitry-sur-Seine, 1945

Rue Emile Zola in Fresnes, 1945

Rue Chabrol in Saint-Denis, 1945

Erik Satie's house in Arcueil, 1945

592

Gentilly, 1943

Saint-Denis, 1945

Gentilly, 1943

Ivry, 1948

Nanterre, 1945

Villejuif, 1945

Cross-country bike race in Gentilly, 1946

600

La Vache Noire, 1946

Suburb to the south, 1949

Orly, 1947

603

604

Arcueil, 1943

Meudon, 1945

606

Saint-Denis, 1943

Daily chore, getting the milk, 1946

608

Rue Marcellin-Berthelot, Choisy-le-Roi, 1945

The back door of Gentilly, 1934

610

Villejuif, 1945

Arcueil, 1944

612

Saint-Denis, 1944

Meudon, 1945

Nogent-sur-Marne, 1945

Monsieur Dubreuil's café in Bagnolet, 1957

616

Puteaux, 1945

617

Arcueil, 1945

Issy-les-Moulineaux, 1949

620

Saint-Denis, 1944

The Gallia Cinema in Gentilly, 1948

Place de la Gare, Ivry-sur-Seine, 1949

Montrouge, 1945

Arcueil, 1945

626

Bagnolet, 1945

Wedding in Montrouge, 1950

Parade for the inauguration of a monument in Cachan, 1947

Montreuil, 1945

630

Float parade in Choisy-le-Roi, 1934

Miss Romainville, 1945

632

Chez Gégène, Quai de Polangis, Joinville-le-Pont, 1946

Bastille Day, 14 July 1945

634

Gentilly, Bastille Day, 14 July 1947

Gentilly, 1949

Demonstration on the Rue Fort in Montrouge, 1949

Le Kremlin-Bicêtre, 1932

639

Vitry-sur-Seine, 1943

Workers' gardens in Fresnes, 1946

L'Haÿ-les-Roses, 1946

642

Villeneuve-Saint-Georges, 1947

Antony, 1946

644

« Un dimanche à la campagne, » 1949 (A Sunday in the country)

645

Bagneux, 1944

646

Circa 1936

647

Vitry, September 1965

648

Essonne, 1945

Choisy-le-Roi, 1946

650

Fresnes, 1945

Montrouge, 1945

652

Nanterre, 1945

653

Villejuif, 1944

655

Vitry, 1945

656

Bois de Vincennes, 1945

On the banks of the Marne, 1945

658

Near Montreuil, 1945

Nogent-sur-Marne, 1945

« Swimming pool » on the Marne, 1945

Joinville-le-Pont, 1934

663

Joinville, March 1949

La Varenne, 1945

Between Joinville and Nogent-sur-Marne, 1945

CHRONOLOGY

Biography
With a few
surprise guests

1912
Born in Gentilly (Val-de-Marne) on 14 April, when the *Titanic*, reputed to be unsinkable, began its fatal plunge in the night, south of the Grand Bank of Newfoundland, after bumping into an iceberg

1918
Mistinguett and Maurice Chevalier put on Jacques Charles' *Pa Ri Ki Ri* at the Casino de Paris (20 October)

1923
Celebrates his solemn First Communion

1925
Passes the entrance competition for the Ecole Estienne in Paris. Learns lithographic engraving, "defunct and out-moded technique that is no longer practised outside the school and which consisted of scratching the surface with a calcareous stone." Receives his diploma as an engraver (in 1929)

1926
In May, the Norwegian Amundsen (1872/1928) flies over the North Pole in an airship

1927
Death of Eugène Atget, in his home at 17 bis, rue Campagne-Première, in the fourteenth arrondissement (4 August). His final request: "I'm dying, go tell my friend Calmettes." His most famous neighbour, Man Ray at number 31.

In New York, in October, beginning of Brancusi vs. the United States trial. The issue: *Oiseau dans l'espace*, a sculpture 1.35 meters high for which American Customs refused to waive import tax, an exoneration customarily granted to works of art. Tax paid by Brancusi: 600 dollars.

Question: "Is *Oiseau dans l'espace* a work of art?" Verdict on 26 November 1928: Yes.

1928
With one of the first Leica models, André Kertész captures (on film), at the same instant, a locomotive passing by on a viaduct and a man with a hat carrying a heavy parcel under his arm

1929
Makes his debut with publicity photographs and drawing designs for the Almann Studio, specialists in pharmaceutical advertising.

In Delfzijl, near Groningue (the Netherlands), Simenon holes up in a houseboat and writes *Pietr-le-Letton*. The hero: Commissioner Maigret

1931
Becomes cameraman for André Vigneau, "painter, illustrator and sculptor" (1 December). Through him will meet Simenon, the Préverts, Maurice Tabard

1932
Sells his first reportage on the Flea Market to *Excelsior*.

1933
Discovers *Paris de nuit* by Brassaï, "inventor of treasures."

1934
Is hired to work at the Renault factory in Boulogne-Billancourt as an industrial photographer. Five years later, he'll be fired for his evident disdain of punctuality. "The factory that I knew was straight out of Zola, greasy rags everywhere, puddles of oil."

1939
Becomes an independent illustrator-photographer, after meeting Charles Rado, founder of the Rapho, Agency...

Glacial public reception of Jean Renoir's *La Règle du jeu*. He would comment, "I was fortunate to have learned to recognize mystification in my youth. In *La Règle du jeu,* I share my discovery with the public, and the world doesn't like it. It upsets their comfort with knowing the truth (Jean Renoir, in *Ma vie et mes films*: Flammarion)

1941
Release of *Citizen Kane,* Orson Welles' first commercial masterpiece. Keyword: "Rosebud."

1942
Illustrates Maximilien Vox's book *Les Nouveaux Destins de l'intelligence française.* Preface: Field Marshal Pétain. "A blooper," he would later confide to the *Magazine Littéraire* (April 1993).

Catches *Le Cheval tombé,* allegory of the German occupation.

1944
Meets Maurice Baquet.

Birth of Sebastião Salgado in Conceição (Brazil)

1946
Joins the Rapho Agency. "His preference for natural light became an obsession. I remember his enthusiasm upon discovering that the Saint-Martin canal underneath the boulevard Richard-Lenoir was lit at regular intervals through circular openings, which in good weather let in a vertical stream of light, similar to that of a film projector in the flies of a theatre. He was so eager to share this enthusiasm with friends!" (Raymond Grosset in *Photo,* October 1995)

Ban on Jean Vigo's *Zero de conduite* is lifted. "Professor, sir, I say, damn you."

1947
Meets Jacques Prévert and Robert Giraud. Christian Dior launches its New-Look

1949
La Banlieue de Paris with a text by Blaise Cendrars is published by Seghers. Signs a contract with the magazine *Vogue* run by Michel de Brunhoff, son of Babar. Photographs Orson Welles at Les Chasseurs café.

Sixteenth International Congress of Psychoanalysis in Zurich, typical example of the Jacques Lacan lambada

1950
Trip to London.

Has a meeting with Colette at her home in the Palais Royal; he admires her collection of paper-weights

1951
Photographs the marriage of the Motillon daughter in Saint-Sauvant (Poitou)

1952
Sortilèges de Paris with a text by François Cali is published by Arthaud.

Brigitte Bardot marries Roger Vadim Plémiannikov (20 Decembre) at the town hall of the fourteenth arrondissement. Honeymoon in Megève at the Auberge de la Gérantière.

Frank Horvat leaves for India (for two years)

1953
Izis' portrait of Paul Iéautaud at Fontenay-aux-Roses

1955
Sabine Weiss is on the set of Jean Renoir's *French Cancan*

1956
Photographs Raymond Queneau "in the twelfth arrondissement of Paris in front of a flower shop selling only blue flowers," as noted in the caption of the *Encyclopaedia Universalis* Corpus 15, page 550, 1985. Receives the Niépce Prize.

Françoise Sagan's *Un certain sourire* comes out. Launching of the so-called Buttes-Chaumont School under the tutelage of Jean d'Arcy, Director of Programming at RTF.

1957
Adopts *Les Enfants de la Place Hébert*

1959
Marcel Bovis teaches aesthetics and colour photography at the Institut Français de Photographie.

Release of Alain Resnais' French film *Hiroshima mon amour* with Emmanuelle Riva and Eiji Okada. Screenplay/script: Marguerite Duras. Time: 90 minutes

1960

Alberto Giacometti writes: "I cannot simultaneously see the eyes, hands and feet of a person standing two or three metres in front of me, but the single part that I do look at carries the feeling of the existence of the whole." (13 February)

1961

Death of comic James Thurber after a life "of a distressing banality," according to Jacques Sternberg. Dorothy Parker is pretty ruffled herself: "It is puzzling, perhaps terrible, to note that James Thurber exercised a veritable influence upon humankind and, one day, he'll have to pay for that."

1962

In New York, thanks to Charles Rado, Jacques-Henri Lartigue meets John Szarkowski, Director of the Photography Department at the MoMA, who discovers his family album. Love at first sight

1963

Staging of *Tontons Flingueurs,* French play by Georges Lautner with Lino Ventura, Bernard Blier, Francis Blanche, Claude Rich. Time: one hour forty minutes.
"We don't know you, but let us tell you that you're setting yourself up for sleepless nights, for a nervousss breakdown!"

1965

Oliviero Toscani leaves the School of Applied Arts in Zurich

1966

Claude Lelouch's *Un homme et une femme* receives the Palme d'or Prize at the Cannes Film Festival.

First French nuclear bomb test in Polynesia (2 July)

1967

Death of Marcel Aymé (14 October)

1968

Leaves for the USSR for *La vie ouvrière* (*The workman's life*)

1970

Alain Juppé enters the National School of Administration (ENA)

1971

Death of Alexandre Vialatte (3 May)

1972

Edouard Boubat travels around Canada with Michel Tournier

1979

Trois secondes d'éternité is published by Contrejour, with 143 photos. "There are days when one experiences the simple act of seeing as a veritable pleasure."

1981

Willy Ronis obtains the Nadar Prize for his collection *Sur le fil du hasard* (Contrejour)

1982

Allows himself to be photographed by François Hers in the Luxembourg Gardens: "I wanted to make an image that would show him as he is: fragile and monumental. I cannot present Paris without thinking of him, he who left his mark on this city and who is for me the greatest modern French photographer. He has only ever shown what it was that he experienced, here and now. He passes through images and goes straight to emotion" (in *Libération,* Tuesday, 10 August, 1982)

Death of Jacques Tati (November 4). Marguerite Duras: "You have to tell it as it is, no one was as beautiful, physically, spiritually, as Tati."

1983

"He concludes that his shyness has prevented him from giving free course to his meanness and from falling into the facility of satire which can scarcely permit, according to him, the making of only 'very closed' photographs. He thinks that photography might have made him less happy, that he might have found less joy in it, if he had been able to use it to express his aggression." Publication of *Doisneau* by Jean-François Chevrier (Belfond), with a cover portrait by Sophie Ristelhueber.

Photographs the filming of Bertrand Tavernier's *Un dimanche à la campagne* with Sabine Azéma.

Death of Louis de Funès (28 January). Michel Cressole: "Louis de Funès died like General de Gaulle, while watching television (…). He's familiar, a local character who has disappeared from our youth. How many hateful family Sunday afternoons he saved us from!"

1984

On assignment for Datar, "a State commission which got me into a real state."

1986

Un certain Robert Doisneau is published by Chêne Editions, dedicated to Barbara Grosset. Sub-title: "The very truthful story of a photographer as told by himself." On page 118, beneath the photo of Jacques Prévert, he writes: "He taught me about the Saint-Martin Canal and also about the word 'tug' which referred to the boat tugging on the slimy chain fixed in the sludge of the canal."

The nuclear reactor at Chernobyl in the Ukraine explodes (26 April, 1:23 am)

1989

"When I jumped into photography, the camera was still made of wood. Today, it has become almost electronic. I still have my nose at the gate with the same curiosity as the very first day." Publication of *A l'imparfait de l'objectif* by Belfond. And of *Doigts pleins d'encre* accompanied by François Cavanna's text, by Hoëbeke Editions

1990

"I remember that when I spoke to you for the first time about photography being a sort of mould of human beings and of things, an imprint that allows them to exist after their actual disappearance or death, you didn't seem as surprised as I had anticipated." Sylvain Roumette writes *Lettre à un aveugle sur des photographies de Robert Doisneau* (Le Tout sur le Tout / Le temps qu'il fait Editions)

1992

Release of Jean-Marie Poiré's *Visiteurs* with Christian Clavier, Jean Reno and Valérie Lemercier. During its broadcast on France 3, on Monday, 1 April 1996, the newspaper *Le Monde* writes: "Heavy-going drama, over-performed. Public triumph." That very night, there were 11,403,600 television viewers.

1993

Question de lumières, a conversation between R.D. and Henri Alekan, is published by Stratem Editions

1994

Doisneau would prefer the label "picture-angler" to that of "picture-hunter," notes *The Independent* upon his death on 1 April. A few days later, Henri Cartier-Bresson writes: "Our friendship is lost in the darkness of time. We will no longer have his laughter filled with compassion, nor his trenchant come-backs and wit, at once funny and profound. Never any needless repetition, a surprise each time. But his deep kindness, his love of people and of a simple way of life will forever be present in his work."

© 1996, 1998 Éditions Hazan
Third edition
© Doisneau/Rapho for the photographs

Translator: Johanna Woll
Design and realization: Atalante, Paris
Editing: Stéphanie Grégoire
Photographs printed by Hervé Hudry, Publimod' photo
Photoengraving: Prodima, Bilbao
Printing: I.G. Castuera, Pampelune

ISBN: 2 85025 529 7
Printed in Spain